EARTH'S LAST FRONTIERS

JUNGLE WORLDS

Ellen Labrecque

Heinemann

LIBRARY

Chicago, Illinois

Edited by Rebecca Rissman, Dan Nunn, and Adrian Vigliano
Designed by Tim Bond
Picture research by Liz Alexander
Originated by Capstone Global Library Ltd

Library of Congress Cataloging-in-Publication Data
Labrecque, Ellen.
  Jungle worlds / Ellen Labrecque.
    pages cm.—(Earth's last frontiers)
  Includes bibliographical references and index.
  ISBN 978-1-4109-6180-8 (hardback)—ISBN 978-1-4109-6185-3 (pa-
perback) 1. Jungle ecology—Juvenile literature. 2. Jungles—Juvenile
literature. I. Title.

QH541.5.J8L33 2014
577.34—dc23   2013013015

Acknowledgments
The author and publisher are grateful to the following for permission to
reproduce copyright material:
Corbis pp. 9 (© Frans Lanting), 14 (© Kevin Schafer/Minden Pictures), 21 (©
Thomas Marent/Minden Pictures), 26 (© Patricio Robles Gil/ Sierra Madre/
Minden Pictures), 27 (© Tim Laman/National Geographic Society), 28 (©
Ocean); Getty Images p. 19 (© 2007 barry b. doyle /Flickr); iStockphoto p.
13 (© Angela Arenal); NASA p. 4; Nature Picture Library pp. 8 (© Nick Gar-
butt), 10 (© Juan Carlos Munoz), 18 (© Roland Seitre), 24 (© Mark Bowler);
Shutterstock pp. 5 (© leungchopan), 7 (© Dr. Morley Read), 12 (© zstock),
15 (© Ralph Loesche), 16 (© Susan Flashman), 17 (© Dr. Morley Read), 20
(AridOcean/NASA), 29 (© Juriah Mosin); SuperStock pp. 22 (Prisma), 23
(Prisma), 25 (age footstock); Design features courtesy of Shutterstock (©
nata_danilenko).

Cover photograph of a river in the jungle reproduced with permission of
Superstock (Alfredo Maiquez/age footstock).

Every effort has been made to contact copyright holders of any material
reproduced in this book. Any omissions will be rectified in subsequent
printings if notice is given to the publisher.

CONTENTS

A FINAL FRONTIER

Jungles cover only about five percent of the Earth's surface. Many parts of these jungles are still a mystery to us. Some have never even been mapped. Let's take a look at this wild world!

WOW!

Jungles are home to more than half of the **species** of plants and animals on Earth.

WHAT ARE THE JUNGLES?

Jungles are found on many continents. Many jungles are found in lowland areas of **river basins**. They are often near the **equator**. This makes their weather hot, wet, and humid.

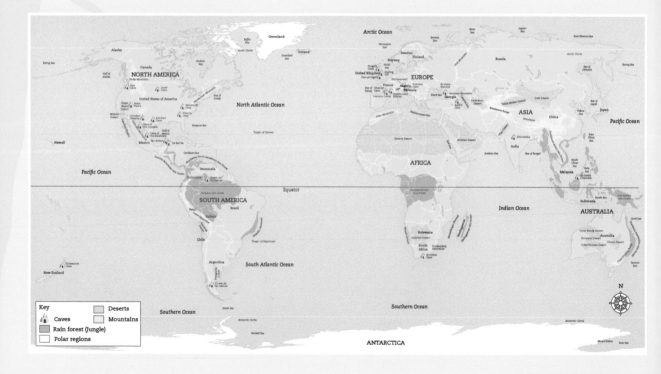

WOW!

The word jungle comes from the Hindi word *jangal*, which means "impossible to enter."

WHY ARE JUNGLES UNEXPLORED?

Thick jungle plants make exploration very difficult. Explorers struggle to enter the forests. Some jungles are also far away. And jungles are filled with dangerous creatures that might attack if they feel threatened.

WOW!

Water is everywhere in a jungle. It drips from leaves, collects in puddles, and runs down mountains. All of this water makes it hard to explore.

JUNGLE LAYERS

There are four levels that form a jungle's **ecosystem**: the forest floor, the **understory**, the **canopy**, and the **emergent layer**. Each layer is home to unique plants and animals.

Emergent layer

Canopy

Understory

Forest floor

11

THE FOREST FLOOR

The forest floor is dark because the trees block sunlight. But don't be fooled! Although it appears lifeless, lizards and some poisonous snakes slither along the forest floor. Fierce animals, such as jaguars, also roam the forest floor looking for lunch.

WOW!

The bushmaster snake's bite releases venom, or poison. Even humans can die from this snake's venom. The snake hides on the forest floor by blending in with the ground.

THE UNDERSTORY

The understory is the space under the leaves, but above the forest floor. Explorers struggle to move through the shrubs, plants, and hanging vines. The understory of the Amazon **rain forest** in South America is some of the thickest jungle in the world.

WOW!

Explorers use a machete, or broad heavy knife, to get through the jungle. They use the knife to hack their way through thick plants and vines.

THE CANOPY

The canopy is high up and very difficult to reach. It is the most unexplored section of the jungle. It is where the treetops form a roof. The canopy is a maze of leaves and branches that take in the sunlight.

WOW!

Explorers string up walkways in the canopy. This is how they explore and study life up here.

THE EMERGENT LAYER

The tallest trees make up the emergent section of the jungle. They grow as high as 200 feet (60 meters). The weather can quickly change from hot and sunny to pouring rain. It can also be very windy. It is almost impossible to explore the emergent.

WOW!

Harpy eagles are the most powerful birds on Earth. They are strong enough to snatch monkeys out of trees to eat them!

THE AMAZON

The Amazon is Earth's largest jungle. Explorers must avoid dangerous wildlife such as alligators and anacondas. The Amazon River is the world's second longest river. It floods during heavy rains. Its powerful currents can even sink ships!

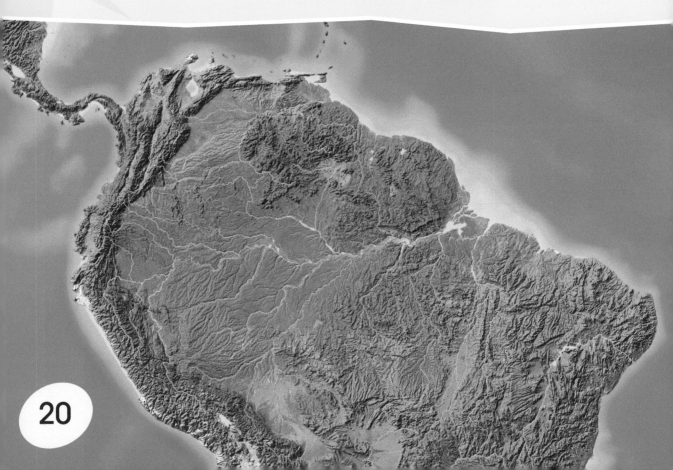

WOW!

Two and a half million different types of insects, tens of thousands of plants, and some 2,000 species of birds and animals live in the Amazon.

THE PEOPLE

Some people who live in jungles have never made contact with the outside world. The Mascho-Piro Indian tribe is one of the last groups that live this way. They are hunters and gatherers. They live off of the plants and animals in the jungle.

WOW!

People of the Embera-Wounaan tribe live in the jungles of Panama.

THE SEARCH FOR MEDICINE

Scientists search jungles for plants that can be used to make medicine. Some jungle plants make chemicals to keep insects and other animals from eating them. These chemicals can be used to make medicines and help sick people.

WOW!

Twenty-five percent of the world's medicines have been discovered in rain forests.

HOW WE EXPLORE

Today, people are exploring all levels of the jungles. Some climb up into the canopy with ropes. Others build platforms and towers to view and study the jungle below. Devices on **satellites** help scientists explore the jungles from above.

WOW!

Scientists stay up on platforms for days on end. They eat and even sleep up there.

ONLY IN THE JUNGLE

If we want to keep exploring the jungles, we must reduce the **deforestation** happening there. This is when people clear out forests. They use the land for things like farming, ranching, and digging for oil. Once the jungle is gone, it is gone forever.

Perhaps in the future, we will know all the secrets of the jungles. Until then, our job is to protect and save them as best as we can!

GLOSSARY

canopy where all of the trees grow together creating a roof over the jungle

deforestation clearing of trees in the jungle

ecosystem community of living and nonliving things that affect each other

emergent layer very top of the canopy; at the top of the tallest trees

equator imaginary line drawn on maps of Earth dividing it into two equal parts

rain forest thick forest with tall trees and a lot of rainfall

river basin area of low-lying land that has been drained by a river

satellite a device that circles the Earth

species living organisms that are very similar to each other and can reproduce

understory in a jungle, the area between the forest floor and the canopy

FIND OUT MORE

There are lots of sources with information on the jungles! You can start with these books and websites.

BOOKS

Alolian, Molly and Bobbie Kalman. *A Rain Forest Habitat*. New York: Crabtree Publishing, 2006.

Greenaway, Theresa. *Eyewitness Jungle*. New York: DK Publishing, 2009.

Marent, Thomas. *Rain Forest*. New York: DK Publishing, 2010.

INTERNET SITES

Facthound offers a safe, fun way to find Internet sites related to this book. All of the sites on Facthound have been researched by our staff.

Here's all you do:
Visit www.facthound.com
Type in this code: 9781410961808

INDEX